Krav Maga

Dominating Solutions to Real World Violence

George Silva

Krav Maga

© Copyright 2015 by George Silva

All rights reserved.

In no way is it legal to reproduce, duplicate, or transmit any part of this document in either electronic means or in printed format. Recording of this publication is strictly prohibited and any storage of this document is not allowed unless with written permission from the publisher. All rights reserved.

The information provided herein is stated to be truthful and consistent, in that any liability, in terms of inattention or otherwise, by any usage or abuse of any policies, processes, or directions contained within is the solitary and utter responsibility of the recipient reader. Under no circumstances will any legal responsibility or blame be held against the publisher for any reparation, damages, or monetary loss due to the information herein, either directly or indirectly.

Respective authors own all copyrights not held by the publisher.

Legal Notice:

This book is copyright protected. This is only for personal use. You cannot amend, distribute, sell, use, quote or paraphrase any part or the content within this book without the consent of the author or copyright owner. Legal action will be pursued if this is breached.

Disclaimer Notice:

Please note the information contained within this document is for educational and entertainment purposes only. Every attempt has been made to provide accurate, up to date and reliable complete information. No warranties of any kind are expressed or implied. Readers acknowledge that the author is not engaging in the rendering of legal, financial, medical or professional advice.

By reading this document, the reader agrees that under no circumstances are we responsible for any losses, direct or indirect, which are incurred as a result of the use of information contained within this document, including, but not limited to, —errors, omissions, or inaccuracies.

Krav Maga

Contents

Page

Introduction..............................7

Chapter 1 – What is Krav Maga?............9

Chapter 2 – The Philosophy and Principles of Krav Maga,.................13

Chapter 3 – Krav Maga and Fitness......23

Chapter 4 – Reasonable Use of Force...33

Chapter 5 – Mastering the Moves.........39

Chapter 6 – The Use of Impact Weapons in Krav Maga......................................54

Chapter 7 - Angry Training...................67

Chapter 8 – Defending Yourself with These Three Moves............................75

Chapter 9 – 5 Krav Maga Moves to Devastate and Dominate......................81

Chapter 10 – Krav Maga Belts..............89

Chapter 11 - The Language of Krav Maga..................99

Chapter 12 – Krav Maga FAQ..............107

Chapter 13 – So You Want to Learn Krav Maga..................113

Conclusion...........................117

George Silva

Introduction

Self-defense is something that everybody should learn, especially in the current climate of terror and random attacks. The instances of attacks on the street has risen significantly in recent times; lack of money, drugs, homophobia, and strong views on race and culture are just some of the reasons why.

Whatever the reason, every single person, man, woman and child, should be prepared and should be able to use reasonable force to defend themselves successfully. While there are plenty of martial arts classes that can teach you certain moves, most of them are only effective when you are defending yourself against another class member, someone who is expecting you to try to fight back.

When you are in the position of a real attack on the streets, there is only one form of self-defense that can help you, only one form that can get you out of trouble with the minimum amount of injury to yourself. That form of self-defense is called Krav Maga.

If you want to learn how to truly defend yourself, read on and find out how Krav Maga can help you to fight back.

Chapter 1

What is Krav Maga?

Krav Maga is most definitely not a pretty form of self-defense and it is not an art in the sense of traditional martial arts. Don't get me wrong; there is absolutely nothing wrong with learning the graceful arts of Tai Chi, or Wing Chun Kung Fu. There is nothing wrong with learning karate, judo or the more commonly known street fighting martial art, Jujitsu. Krav Maga leaves all that grace behind at the door and takes you out onto the street to teach very simple but aggressive movements that punch straight to the heart of self-defense.

Krav Maga is a Hebrew word, which means "close combat". It was developed for the Israeli military by Imi Lichtenfield when the military decided that they needed a combat system that was hand-to-hand, a system that could be learned very quickly and would be highly effective, no matter your age, gender, athletic type or body type. The system was developed in an environment that was hostile, not allowing combatants to devote many hundreds of hours to learning hand-to-hand combat. Krav Maga has no set rules, no forms and no specific combinations of moves as a reaction to an attack. The training focuses on simple techniques for self-defense using the natural reactions of the body.

Unlike other styles or systems of fighting, Krav Maga is a system of survival, a system that deals with safety issues on a personal basis. It is a modern system one that is highly refined, a method that is designed for use against attackers that are armed or unarmed and for use against multiple attackers at once.

Most self-defense methods use techniques - Krav Maga does not. Instead, it is based on principles and it is important that you understand the difference between technique and principle. Methods that are driven by technique do not allow for any variation in an attack. They do not allow for any reactions to a counterattack, the type of body that you have, your physical limitations, the environment of the attack and may other variables that are likely to be present during a violent attack.

Krav Maga is what we call an integrated system. This mean that the techniques you will be taught can be used in many different situations. You will not be taught one technique for one situation because that is not the nature of the real world. Instead, you will be able to learn a number of reactions that can be used in many different kinds of attack. Krav Maga is not a martial art and it is not a combination of other forms of self-defense and styles. It is a carefully researched system, allowing for harmony throughout, from the very basic starting point right through to the most advanced levels.

Unlike other methods of self-defense, Krav Maga is fully battle-tested and the training involves pressure testing to improve your chances of survival in the street. Stress drills are used in the training, a very vital part of the pressure testing system. The stress drills are designed to loosely replicate the stress of a real-life violent combat situation – mentally, physically and emotionally.

Krav Maga continues to grow in popularity as more people are finding that it is the best form of self-defense. It is the perfect combination of real-world self-defense, a practical method that is also challenging and a fun alternative to regular fitness regimes. More than

200 law enforcement agencies have already adopted Krav Maga in their combat training regimes and there are more than 200 affiliated Krav Maga schools in the US alone.

Chapter 2

The Philosophy and Principles of Krav Maga

The ultimate aim of Krav Maga is to teach you problem solving. While it was originally developed as a way of addressing violent attacks and encounters, the philosophy can also be used in many other parts of your daily life. Krav Maga is a no-frills system, one that is designed to instill in you a fighting spirit, a mindset that is aggressive and a sense of accomplishment. While Krav Maga recognizes that self-defense is not used as a form of punishment, the ultimate goal is to ensure that you make it home safely, in one piece and, in that sense, the best way to achieve that is through a decisive and aggressive reaction.

The main principle is that you do not get hurt while defending yourself. While this might seem like something that is fairly obvious, it is far-reaching and dictates that you should actually go to great lengths to avoid conflict where possible. Krav Maga is not about weighing into any situation, kicking and punching. It is about deciding the best course of action and the foremost course should be to walk away unharmed and without having to defend yourself.

That is not always possible but a good understanding of violence and people who are violent should heighten your awareness and your ability to avoid conflict. If you cannot get out of a situation unharmed then you must learn that your defense has to be aggressive in order to get rid of the threat. You must be able to neutralize the attacker and cut the chances of you being injured.

To do this you must train from a position of definite disadvantage. Even the most steadfast of trainees can become distracted; that is life. It doesn't matter whether it is a momentary lapse in concentration, apathy or complacency, it will happen and it is a natural happening. Krav Maga training takes the realities of life into consideration and will force you to train from a weak position, a position in which you are not ready or prepared for attack.

Real life dictates that you will not be ready for an attack on the street and the Krav Maga training takes this into account, training you to defend yourself from a neutral position. Doing this forces you to perform techniques without paying attention to learning the proper footwork, balance, hand positioning and weight distribution. If Krav Maga is to be truly effective in real-life situations, the techniques taught must not rely on you being prepared or early in the defense. This is one of the most significant parts to Krav Maga training – you must learn to identify and to eliminate any immediate danger. If you cannot address the root cause, there is no technique on earth that will be successful. In most case, much time is lost on addressing peripheral issues instead of getting straight to the heart of the matter. Krav Maga teaches you to address the most imminent danger up front, and it teaches you to address that danger efficiently and effectively. It teaches you to use the natural instincts of your body.

Many of the self-defense methods taught today teach you techniques that may be seen as being better under a specific circumstance but most of these methods do not work in harmony with your natural body rhythms or reactions. They also require an extensive period of training. These techniques are more likely to fail when you are faced with the very real stress of a very real violent encounter. Krav Maga training recognizes that your natural fine motor skills are not likely to be effective when combined with the rush of adrenaline that comes with stress. Instead, Krav Maga teaches you to use your body naturally, in a way that your body would react, not in the way that you have forced it to react. The benefits of these techniques are two-fold. Firstly, you are more likely to be successful during a real-life attack and, secondly, the length of time needed to train is much less than in other, more common forms of defense training.

Krav Maga training focuses on the average person and their abilities and, because of that, it is not practical to undergo months and months of training. It takes into account that the way your body responds to violence or fear can fall into one of three categories- fight, flight or freeze. Krav Maga training uses drills that encourage a decisive reaction when your body is under stress, moving you from a state of being unable to do anything to a state where you naturally defend yourself, efficiently and effectively.

The next principle is to learn to be effective in your dealings with any secondary danger in the attack. You need to understand that the most important factor in any successful defense is the identification and elimination of the immediate threat. However, you must also understand that secondary dangers can result from any attack, whether they are because of the original attack or simply a by-product. Either way, the best way to mitigate a secondary attack effectively is to use sound tactics and to apply the key principles of Krav Maga effectively. That means being able to simultaneously be explosive, defend and counterattack. Your counterattack must be carried out as soon as possible, the most preferable situation being that the counter attack is performed at the same time as the defense to the original attack.

Strong counterattacks are a vital part of a defense that works. Using strength and aggression in your counterattack is the best way to cause maximum disruption to the attack because it forces your attacker to have to react to you. Instead of having the upper hand, instead of being the attacker, they now find that they have to defend themselves against you, instead of being able to continue with their attack or increase the aggression they are using against you. The earlier you deliver the counterattack, the quicker your attacker has to shift into becoming a defender. Remember this – nearly every criminal is looking for someone to be a victim. They are not looking for their victim to fight back and an aggressive counterattack that is performed almost immediately will give you the element of surprise and nock your attacker off balance, both physically and metaphorically. Defense alone will not win the fight.

Another sound principle of Krav Maga is that you should attack in vulnerable areas. Krav Maga teaches you that a good system of self-defense does not rely solely on your ability to fight off an attacker based on your own physical attributes. It also teaches you that you should attack vulnerable parts of the body in your counterattack. Those parts include the eyes, the liver, the groin, the jaw, the throat, the kidneys, the fingers, the shins, the knees and the insteps. Striking these areas will give you the opportunity to cause maximum damage with minimum effort and minimum strength.

You should always use the environment to your advantage. This means being able to quickly analyze your environment. A violent attack will very rarely occur in an environment that is controlled. Therefore, your Krav Maga training will teach you how to evaluate the environment quickly so that you can use the best form of defense applicable. For example, if you were attacked on a terrain that is unstable, slippery or uneven, you should choose an upper body strike, rather than an over-kick as this will serve to knock your attacker off their balance. You will also be taught to use objects that you find at the scene of the attack. You can use blunt objects in an offensive manner by striking with them or you can use objects such as chairs in a defensive manner, to protect yourself an increase your survival chances. As fights are never fair, this is an important principle to remember. If your attacker is intent on causing you maximum harm, you must do whatever you deem to be necessary and that means using whatever is available to defend yourself and attack your attacker. This applies in all cases, no matter what the advantages or disadvantages are at that moment in time.

Fight are very much dynamic and the variable will be shifting constantly. Krav Maga teaches that a defender must do whatever is needed to ensure that they can go home safely.

One of the biggest mindsets that Krav Maga teaches is that you must not quit. Your training will go to immense lengths, taking you through stress drills that are specially designed, to teach you to harness a fighting spirit. In a real-life situation, it is vital that you recognize the signs of potential violence early and that you also recognize that is imperative that you mitigate any possible variations. There are any number of factors that can affect the outcome of a violent attack and most of these will initially be controlled by the attacker. The one factor that you will have is your fighting spirit and it is this that you must cultivate and nurture if you are to successfully defend yourself and fight back. In the military, this is known as cognitive dissonance, or to learn that attitude always follows behavior. The stress drills in Krav Maga are designed to empower your physically and emotionally, kick-starting the skill set that is needed to perform when you are under great stress and under duress. The true essence of Krav Maga, the one thing that will save you, is your willingness to do whatever is necessary to survive. You must have a strong "never say die" attitude in order to be able to successfully adapt no matter what the situation, and be able to come through a violent encounter safely.

The ultimate goal in any confrontation is that you are able to walk away and go home in safety. To that end, the next principle is, quite simply, to flee to a safe place. Your Krav Maga training will teach you that you must defend ad counterattack aggressively to eliminate the threat. However, it is also vital that you do not hang around in the way of harm for any longer than is absolutely necessary. As time goes by in a confrontation, the variables increase, and that means that there is a big chance of other attackers joining in, of weapons being introduced, of injury and fatigue. Each confrontation, each attack is unique. The situation is going to define the reaction and that includes knowing when it is right to make a safe escape. In all cases, the defender should be looking to get away from the scene of the confrontation, to a safe place as quickly as they possibly can.

The final Krav Maga principle to learn is that you must never do any more than is absolutely necessary. The goal of the training is to help to enhance your chances of survivability. Out of pure necessity, Krav Maga is aggressive and it is forceful. However, these are words that we use to describe a system of self-defense and self-defense should never ever be used as a system of punishment. To eliminate the threat against you, you should do no more than what is absolutely necessary to facilitate your safe escape from the situation. When you are in a position of defending yourself, it is not OK, nor is it acceptable to use your Krav Maga training to exact revenge upon your attacker. Not only is this morally unacceptable, it is not sound in a tactical sense, simply because you are risking staying too long at the scene and that increases the chances of the other variables entering the fight. The best solution is extrications, as quickly and as safely as possible.

Chapter 3

Krav Maga and Fitness

When we talk about fitness in relation to Krav Maga, it must be fitness that is combat functional. By that, I mean that all the drills, the exercises and the methods you will be taught are designed in such a way that they enhance the physical tools that are vital to improving your performance in self-defense.

The exercises that you should include in your regime must replicate, as closely as possible, the movements that are used in self-defense training and each exercise must have a specific goal. For the purposes of Krav Maga training, combat functional exercises must address, as an absolute minimum, stamina, explosiveness, strength training and flexibility. Krav Maga uses unique training methods and, very often, students find that they have achieved a physique they never thought possible, a confidence they never had before and fitness levels that were always out of their reach.

The Krav Maga trainers are professional self-defense trainers and it is their goal to give you the tools necessary for personal safety. Krav Maga is totally different from a gym-training regime in that, not only do you get a sculpted body, you get the tactics and the life-saving techniques to go with it.

Strength training is not about aesthetics and must not be confused with bodybuilding. Strength training is focused solely on being able to increase your strength, not your size and it is most definitely not about cultivating a look. Strength training is firmly focused on either developing or enhancing your athletic attributes and, while there are plenty of ways to increase strength, not all methods work the same. In Krav Maga training, you will find that some methods are used more than others are as they are more preferred.

When we talk about strength training in relation to Krav Maga, we are talking about the ability to augment your capacity to damage a person attacking you as well as your ability to absorb the punishment meted on you. Krav Maga emphasizes the need for aggression in counterattacks as we as being able to perform from a disadvantageous position. This can include defending yourself after you have been struck or at the time you are being struck.

Explosiveness is the ability to produce vast amounts of strength and effort in a very short period of time. While explosiveness is related to strength training physical strength does not always equate to explosiveness. We normally use the word plyometrics to describe the exercises that are used to develop your explosiveness and these exercises have one common goal – to increase how much force is applied and decrease the time in which it takes to apply that force. In most of the Krav Maga defenses, the biggest equalizer is being able to perform explosively. Because you dispatch the force in a rapid manner, rather than gradually, an explosive reaction can help to mitigate the chances of your attacker being able to react and adjust to your defense and counterattacks. This is an incredibly important aspect of Krav Maga because it allows the smaller defender to perform adequately against a larger attacker.

Flexibility is important in Krav Maga because the method does not rely on fancy techniques, nor does it emphasize or encourage them. Flexibility is defined as an increase in the range of motion and it is vital for a person to reach the maximum potential in all of their techniques, especially combative techniques.

Range of motion is generally described as the distance that a person can achieve between a flexed position and the extended position of any specific muscle or joint group. An increase in flexibility is important to help minimize the chances of injury and to increase speed and power because it allows the muscles and the joints to extend fully.

Endurance, or stamina, is being able to exert the maximum effort, or as near to maximum effort as possible, over a longer period of time. This is achieved through aerobic or anaerobic training. Most aggressive confrontations actually last less than 60 seconds but endurance or stamina training is a vital part of any fitness regime, not just Krav Maga. When you are involved in a violent confrontation, the stress that accompanies the encounter, together with the physical response that is required, will cause rapid fatigue in your body. Fitness training ha to include an endurance aspect, allowing you to condition both your mind and body to be able to exert the maximum effort for longer, for as long as it takes to eliminate the threat and get away safely.

As well as this, because nearly all violent encounters are uncertain, tense and evolve at a rapid pace, the dynamics will change. This means that, when new threats are introduced, you must have the stamina needed to continue the fight.

Once you have made the firm decision to start Krav Maga training, there are certain things that you must keep in mind if you are to have the best training experience possible. Your Krav Maga instructor should also go over these considerations with you.

First, you must be prepared for each training session. This means you must be physically, mentally and emotionally prepared if you are to get the most out of each session. Make sure that you seek advice from your physician to make sure that you can safely undergo Krav Maga training. You must also consider a diet that will help to optimize the training. The best way to give your body the fuel to undergo each session is to eat a meal that is rich in carbohydrates about three or four hours before the training. To give yourself an extra boost, eat a snack that is easily digestible about an hour before the session. Most sessions will last about an hour so you must ensure that you are adequately hydrated throughout. Drink plenty of water throughout the day and throughout the entire training session.

A typical Krav Maga training session will start with a warmup, followed by combative training, self-defense training and stress drills. The warmups are designed to help prepare you, physically and mentally, for the hard training you are about to go through. However, regardless of the content of the warmups, nobody knows your body better than you do. If there are specific areas that you feel need attention, such as stretching, make sure that you address these areas before the session starts. It is also very important that you let your Krav Maga trainer know if you have any injuries beforehand as this can affect your training.

Spend time preparing yourself mentally before you start. In the same way that your trainer will help you to prepare physically, he or she can also give you some mental techniques to use. Spend some time thinking about the session ahead, about the goals you want to achieve. Just showing up for the training session is a huge step but it is better to have specific goals, as well as the understanding that putting in the maximum amount of effort will result in the maximum results and ensuring that you are getting the absolute best out of your training sessions.

One of the most important parts of the training is to ensure that your knuckles and wrists are protected during hard punching exercises. There are lots of ways that you can wrap your hands to help with this and this is one of the most practical ways to do it:

1. Relax your hand completely and spread out your fingers

2. Place the thumb lop of the wrap around the thumb and draw the wrap over the back of your hand

3. Wrap it around your wrist two or three times, making sure it is two to three inches up from the joint of the wrist. This ensures that you get the proper support. Make sure that the wrap is snug and firm and is not twisted.

4. From your wrist, draw the wrap over the back of your hand, in the direction of your wrist, and then go around the hand. Repeat the x-pattern at least two more times, if not three.

5. Continue wrapping round your palm to the base of your thumb, wrap round the thumb and go back towards the wrist, on the side of your palm.

6. Wrap it around your thumb once more

7. From the thumb, go over the back of your hand and take the wrap in between your ring and little fingers

8. Take the wrap around your palm towards the wrist

9. Repeat this for all of the fingers on your hand but not the thumb

10. Once you have done the last finger, bring the wrap across your palm towards the wrist and go over the back of your hand towards your knuckles.

11. Wrap around the top of the knuckles and continue over the back of your hand towards the wrist

12. Use the rest of the wrap to go around your wrist and then fasten the loop and the hook

The environment in which you are training will be controlled as much as is humanly possible. If you are attending sessions at a licensed Krav Maga facility, control is normal but it is still down to y to ensure that you are diligent and understand any potential or inherent dangers. Remove any obstacles that are not relevant to the training session and check the equipment that is being used to ensure its integrity. If you are training outside, scan the area to identify and remove any potential hazards. If you are not at a licensed Krav Maga training facility, be sure that you have a full first aid kit close to hand while you are training.

There are certain items that are essential to your training experience. If you are taking part in combative training, there are a number of pads that you can use to help enhance the training session. The punch pad, often known as the tombstone pad is one of the most versatile and can be used to practice upper body kicks and combatives.

The kick shield pad is perfect for training on some of the stronger kicks that are used in Krav Maga and is also useful for practicing knee attacks. It is a piece of equipment that you will find in use in many drills.

Focus mitts are used in advanced and intermediate training, especially when training to use the punches. To make the most out of your session, to train as hard as you can while keeping injuries to the minimum, there are a number of essential pieces of equipment – hand wraps, mouthpieces, gloves and groin protection are all vital. However, you should also learn to train without this equipment. After all, you won't be able to wrap your hands and slot a mouthpiece in when you are face with a real-world confrontation. Training without the protective gear should only be done under supervised and controlled environments.

Chapter 4

Reasonable Use of Force

One of the most asked questions is, "will I get into trouble with the law if I use self-defense tactics against an attacker?" This is a very valid question but there is no clear-cut answer. How right your actions are will depend entirely on the situation and the context in which they are used. Before I go on with this subject, we must first understand the difference between civil complaints and criminal charges. Unfortunately, we live in a society that is deeply litigious and it seems that lawsuits can be brought against a person by just about anybody for just about anything This is ant actually strictly true because a judge will usually throw out any case that is frivolous and a waste of time.

However, when you start your self-defense training, you should know this – even if your use of self-defense is reasonable for the situation, and both the district attorney and the police are in complete agreement, your attacker s perfectly able to file a civil suit against you. However, this doesn't mean that he or she will win but you will most likely have to pay out for legal representation to prove that you were justified. Criminal cases must adhere to much higher standards; the police have to collect the evidence and make the decision on whether to arrest any of the participants of the altercation (and that includes you). The evidence must be reviewed by the district attorney to decide what, if any, crime has been committed and if there is sufficient evidence to move to a trial.

All law enforcement and justice agents must use their own judgment but they are still guided by practices and laws that are established and predictable. However, those laws vary depending on which State you are in and the policies vary from one county to the next. It is not within the scope of this book to list all the guidelines for each State and each county but I can talk about general guidelines.

First off, you must understand that you cannot hurt someone just because you think that they deserve to get hurt. For example, let's say that you are attacked and you defend yourself while, at the same time, delivering a hard kick to his groin. If that single kick is enough to incapacitate your attacker, you are not allowed, by law, to continue harming him. You cannot weigh in with a few more kicks and punches just because you think he should be beaten for attacking you. The law allows for a certain amount of self-defense but it does not allow for retribution.

Depending on the situation, you are allowed to do whatever is necessary to keep safe but no more than that. Often, we hear of people who have been attacked and use self-defense, saying that they were fearing for their lives. While this may be appropriate, it is not sufficient enough to warrant viciously attacking someone when they are done, or "for the hell of it". It comes down to this – what you feel s only one factor that is taken into consideration. For all anyone knows, you could be a paranoid schizophrenic, someone who is always living in fear for his or her life. The standard to which you can be held in the United States is: ***You are allowed to use whatever force a reasonable person, in your situation, would feel is necessary to protect himself.***

The key word in that sentence is "reasonable", a word that gives a situation a certain amount of objectivity. Let's say that a man who stands 6 foot tall approaches a woman who is much smaller, in a dark parking lot, grabbing her by the throat. In that situation, a reasonable person would most certainly feel threatened and could respond with an aggressive level of self-defense to ensure they stay safe. If, on the other hand, the smaller woman was to attack a 6 foot tall man, it would be reasonable to assume that the man would need to use much less force to subdue the situation and protect himself.

Please note, this does not mean that the man cannot defend himself, it is just assumed that he would be more restrained in his defense. Of course, it all comes down to details and it is those details that have the final say on the opinion of a reasonable person. For example, let's assume that the woman is a fully trained martial artist and the man is struggling with a broken leg. It would be reasonable to assume that the man could take a more aggressive stance in this situation. If he were the one doing the attacking, he would expect the woman to defend herself, and retreat from the situation, instead of smacking his head into the ground repeatedly.

There is a line, a point at which self-defense becomes the use of excessive force and, in that situation, it would be down to the woman to explain why she felt it was reasonable to attack repeatedly with such force.

Both the district attorney and the police would use the Reasonable Man standard or something similar and would take the entire situation and all of the details and specifics into account when determining whether or not to file criminal charges. When it comes to law enforcement the use of force standards is a little different purely because of the nature of their job. In general, a law enforcement officer is allowed to use force that is one level higher than that of the assailant in order to control the situation and make the arrest. Civilians are not there to arrest suspects but they can use reasonable force to defend themselves but not more force than is absolutely necessary.

The biggest message that Krav Maga training give you is to use no more force than you absolutely need to but be prepared and, indeed, willing, to do whatever is necessary to ensure your safety.

Krav Maga

Chapter 5

Mastering the Moves

Learning Krav Maga is about so much more than the physical techniques but they are a vital part and, in this chapter, I am going to talk about some of the more basic type of moves and defenses that Krav Maga entails:

Upper Body strikes and Defenses

Any strike will have plenty of force behind it provided you combine an acceleration of speed with a total shift in body weight as you push your weapons through your opponent, your weapons being your hands and arms in this case. The very best way to practice this is to take it in stages, just like with any technique. Each stage of the technique has to be isolated from all the others and then practiced to perfection. As you gain mastery of all the stages separately, you can then combine them into one single technique. Practice in front of a mirror so that you can see your form and monitor it, correcting where necessary.

You can use a number of different parts of your body as weapons, including your arms, forearms, hands, elbows, shins, knees and your head. There is a clear advantage in being able to use the hardest parts of your body, like your feet, knees and elbows, as weapons against the softer vulnerable parts of your attacker's body.

Those softer parts include the eyes, the groin and the throat, all vulnerable parts of the body and attacking these is one very good way to end a fight. It is these targets that we emphasize when learning Krav Maga. You already know your own body's sensitive pot; if you manage to poke yourself in the eye, even lightly, you will feel your eyeball tense up and water; if you manage to hit yourself in the groin, perhaps by landing over a bicycle bar in the wrong way, you already know what it feels like and, if you were to tap yourself in the throat, you will feel the sensation straight away.

Do keep in mind that, if you were to strike hard at your attacker's throat, you can do some serious damage, in some cases, fatal. This is why one of the first things you are taught is to protect your own throat at all costs, as well as other important body parts. The strikes I am going to talk about in this chapter are only a tiny number of those that are there to learn, and they must only ever be used if you are in genuine fear for your life or for a limb.

These kinds of strikes are generally taught from intermediate Krav Maga level and upward. As with any other upper body strike, the movement of your hips and weight are vital o that you can take full advantage of the core strength of your mass and body and to deliver full reach and full power. You must also ensure that the hand or arm you are striking with are properly aligned and positioned.

It doesn't matter which type of upper body strike you use, moving your body weight forwards is going to allow you put all of your weight behind your strike, resulting in a greater force when you connect with your target. The following are tips for striking out effectively:

- Make use of your whole body. When you strike, move your whole body, and use your entire torso. As you do, as your strength and body weight push the strike, you will gain maximum effect on the impact.

- Don't forget to breathe! As the strike is delivered, exhale. Some people scream out when they hit, it has the same effect – it will prepare you and your body for the strike, both delivering it and receiving one. Exhaling or screaming allows oxygen to be transferred into your muscles and it helps to keep your movements under control. It also creates a vacuum inside your lungs that helps you to defend against counterstrikes to the middle of your body.
- Aim for a vulnerable target. You will most definitely gain more effect for the effort if you target the most vulnerable parts of the body.

Straight Punches – Front and Rear

These strikes are core upper body strikes that target the throat, jaw or nose, three of the most vulnerable areas if the body.

Stand in left outlet stance keeping your ands curled into loose fists. Pivot the rear heel out. Remember not to jump with both feet at the same time as you will most definitely lose your stability. There should be a very brief pause in between steps s you launch your whole body forward, punching your hip through the strike. At the same time, push your left arm out, punching your fist towards your attacker. As your arm reaches out, tighten up your fist and, when you make contact, make sure that your palm is parallel to the ground. Raise your left shoulder up and tuck in your chin to provide protection to your jaw and your neck. After the strike, return back to your original stance. Practice this using an open hand to start with and by simulating pushing someone, the motion that you would go through. Then practice the exact same moves with your fist closed The idea is to refine the process and refine the natural motion of your body.

For a rear punch, stand in left outlet with your hands loosely fisted, Turn your right leg on the ball of your foot very slightly as your push your hips, your right shoulder and your right arm forwards. Tuck in your chin to your right shoulder as a way of protecting it from a strike. Again, when you practice this, practice by simulating pushing with an open hand and then with a closed fist. To practice this, start off by allowing both of your hands to dangle down loosely at your side. As you lift and extend your arms out in a natural move, allow your hips to pivot. Once you are comfortable with this, move on to making the proper fist and executing punches.

Over-the-Top Punch

This punch is one that attacks from a slight vertical angle, allowing you to slam your fist down on your opponent's jaw, nose or eye-socket. The movement of your body is very similar to that of the over-the-top-elbow, with your striking arm moving from a high point to a low one, slamming down on to your opponent. This is a very effective move when you are in a position to trap your opponent' forward arm with yours, bringing his defense down and delivering the punch to his head, which is now exposed.

Front Straight Web Strike

This strike is fast and direct and, if you use it, aim directly for the throat, specially aiming for your opponent's windpipe. Provided you are accurate and your timing is right, for a first strike, this one can be pretty devastating.

Web strikes use the webbing on your hand, in between the thumb and the forefinger, to deliver a strike to the throat and windpipe. Keeping your hand parallel with the ground, you are creating a striking tool that is thin, strong and capable of getting in under the chin of your opponent.

Stand in left outlet or fighting stance with your hands curled into loose fists. In a similar way to how you start a straight punch, step your left foot forward and draw the rear heel quickly in and back a little. Again, you are not jumping both feet together here, there should be the briefest of pauses between the two steps as you launch your whole body forward. Extend out your left arm and thrust the web of you and in to your opponent's throat. Make contact, keeping your palm parallel to the ground and raise up your left shoulder, tucking in your chin to protect our own neck and throat. Keep your non-dominant hand up, providing farther protection to your own body and be prepared to follow this attack with another combative move. After the strike, return to your original stance.

It is important that you accurate and that you are very careful with this – if you do not hit right, with the bone and the web just under your index finger, you run a real risk of breaking your own thumb. This s a move that requires a great deal of practice so try it on your own thigh, at a point just above your kneecap to make sure you know how your hand has to be positioned.

Rear Straight Web Strike

This is another move that you should aim at your opponent's throat and windpipe. Start as you did with the front web strike, keeping your hands loosely curled into fists. Pivot on the ball of your right leg slightly, as if you were pushing through a wall or something similar. Push your hips, right shoulder and the web of your right hand into the throat of your opponent. Keep your chin tucked in to protect your own throat and shoulder and keep your other hand up in a protective position.

Drill – Combination Punch and Web Strike

Combination drills give you practice at both the straight punch and the web strike together. Starting with a straight punch will knock your attackers head back, exposing his or her throat at which point you go in with the web strike, straight at the exposed area.

To practice the drill, get your partner to hold a small target pad facing you straight on o the larger surface area of the pad is exposed. After the punch has been delivered your partner should immediately turn the pad so the thin edge is facing you, giving you the narrow surface that will simulate the throat. Here's the drill:

- Start in left outlet stance
- Execute 2 straight punches and 20 right rear web strikes

- Repeat, starting from outlet stance, 20 times
- From both the left and right outlet stances create combinations and vary them

Thinking through the different combination will help you on your way to mastering the Krav Maga techniques.

Knuckle Edge Strike

This is a very fast strike that should be aimed directly at the throat and windpipe of your opponent and it is a strike that is normally set up by a previous combative move. It is very similar to the web strike except that you are using the knuckles and curled fingers in the same position that you would use them to knock on a door.

Your upper body movements and lower body movements are exactly the same as they are for the straight punch and the web strike with the only exception being that you use a different area of your hand. The same way you do with the web strike, ensure that you hand is aligned properly. Get this right and you will deliver a devastating blow.

Drill – Combination Punch and Knuckle Edge Strike Combination

This drill is similar to the previous combination using the straight punch and the knuckle edge strike. As with the last combination, the straight punch will knock the opponent off balance, throwing their head back and exposing the throat for you to go in with the knuckle edge strike. Again, you should practice this with a partner holding a hand pad up.

The pad should be held so that the largest area faces you for both of these strikes. Be very careful when you execute the knuckle edge strike on the pad – the strike is aimed at soft tissue and some of the hand held target pads are a little hard and not very forgiving. The last thing you want to do is hurt yourself in practice. Here's the drill:

- Start at the left outlet stance
- Execute 20 straight punches and 20 right knuckle edge trike
- Return to the left outlet stance and repeat 20 times
- From left and right outlet stance, create new combinations and vary them

As with the last drill, this will help you to master the techniques

Straight Front Forearm Strike

This short sharp direct strike should be aimed at the nose, jaw or throat. Using the right footwork and your full body weight, this is a very powerful for knocking back your attacker, particularly if you aim for the throat area.

Stand in left outlet, keeping your hand curled up to loose fist. Step forward on your left foot while, at the same time, bringing your left arm up parallel to your chest. This exposes the outer edge of the forearm. The upper body and lower body moves are similar to those in the web strike, right rear straight punch and knuckle edge strikes, except for the area that you are targeting.

As your forearm extends out to execute the strike, tighten up your fist and step forward to throw your full body weight behind the strike. Make sure that you step with both of your feet and that you thrust off from the ball of your rear foot. Raise up your left shoulder and tuck in your chin to protect your neck and jaw. Keep your other hand up to protect yourself and be prepared to launch a further combative if needs be. After the strike is executed, return to the left outlet stance

Straight Rear Forearm Strike

In this move, you use your forearm to target your opponent's throat, jaw or nose using your rear right arm. Starting in the left outlet stance, curl your fists into a loose fist. Pivot the right leg a little on the ball of your foot as you push your hips, rear right shoulder and the outer forearm, dropping it perpendicular, towards your opponent. Tuck in your chin to protect your shoulder and throat from attack and keep your left hand up to protect yourself. Be prepared to launch a further combative if needed. Once the strike has been executed, return immediately to left outlet stance.

Drill – Forearm Strike Combination

This drill gives you plenty of opportunity to practice and is very effective at knocking your opponent back. You can do this in three ways – with a heavy punch bag to develop your power, with a partner to develop accuracy and a mirror to review your overall technique. Here's the drill:

- Start from left outlet stance
- Alternate 20 left and 20 right rear forearm strikes
- Move to right outlet stance and repeat the drill

- Back to left outlet stance and execute 20 left forearm and 20 right rear web strikes, or you can do knuckle edge trikes
- Switch to right outlet stance and repeat.
- From both left and right, create combinations and vary them

Clothesline Strike

Use this strike to aim directly for your opponent's throat. To do this, step forward and to the side of your opponent. Make sure your elbow is bent slightly otherwise you will cause yourself an injury when you hyperextend the elbow. Use your inner forearm, the thumb side, to thrust forward into the throat.

You can proactive this with a partner holding a hand or a kicking pad or you can use a heavy bag. If you use a partner, make sure they hold the pad out and away from their own face so that they done put themselves at risk of being struck in the face with the bone that is just under the pointer finger – this s known as a ridge-hand strike.

Chapter 6

The Use of Impact Weapons in Krav Maga

While Krav Maga primarily teaches you to use the natural forces and reactions of your body, it will also teach you how to use and how to defend yourself against impact weapons. These weapons can be in any number of forms – a hammer, a baton, a crowbar, a chair, or anything that can be used as a weapon against someone. In Krav Mage, impact weapons and edged weapons are referred to as "cold weapons" and attacks with them can come from any direction, from up on high or down low, from any angle in single-swing attack. There are three fundamental principles of defense – to close the distance while deflecting an attack, to disengage until you can see the correct time to close the distance and to retreat immediately.

Close the Distance

Whichever weapon is used, the end of it is where the most fore is generated from. This is because the wrist acts as a fulcrum. This means that the most dangerous point of the attack is to be struck with the end of the weapon. The momentum of an object decreases the closer you get to the swinging wrist of your assailant. In an optimal situation, the distance between the attacker and the defender can be closed up before the weapon comes into use and the assailant can be debilitated with combative moves, blocking their access to their weapon, while taking control of the situation.

If the weapon is successfully deployed and brought into the fight, if the defender can close the distance between him or herself and the assailant, he or she can block or, at the very least, redirect the weapon with body defenses in most cases. At the same time, they can use counterattacks that will knock the assailant back. In all Krav Maga defenses, the hand is always the leading point. It leads the body to deflect and/or redirect the weapon while counterattacking at the same time.

Time Correctly

One of the biggest part to a successful defense is having precise timing – knowing how to close the distance and how to use the right tactic at the right time. Fight timing is often considered to be a fusion of your own instinct and decision making, be it to preempt an attack, move out of the way, deflect and redirect the weapon, control it and strike or retreat. In simple terms, it is a way of harnessing the natural instinct of your body's movements while making or grabbing the opportunity to end the encounter with whatever tactic you can. You, the defender, will attack your assailant. The techniques and the tactic taught to you in Krav Maga training are properly designed to give you the capability to preempt the attack before a weapon of any description can be brought into the fight. The goal is to stop your assailant from getting in there first. You will learn to recognize body language and intent to both literally and figuratively stop him in his tracks.

Retreat Immediately

As soon as you can see that the threat has been eliminated, or at least stopped in its tracked, you must get out of the way to safety before any more attacks are forthcoming.

Below, we are going to take a look at using an overhand one-handed strike using a blunt object to defend yourself against an attack with an impact weapon.

Typically, an attack with a blunt weapon comes from an overhead swing. In this technique, we will assume that the assailant is using his right hand and the defender is face to face with him. The defense should be executed with the left arm and counterpunches given with the right arm. You left arm will be controlling the weapon as well.

You goal here is to close up the distance between you and your assailant to intercept the weapon and then redirect or deflect it over your shoulder. At the same time, you will deliver a punch to your assailant's throat, nose or jaw, simultaneously trapping the arm with the weapon so that you can remove it from his or her grip.

A good way to practice the deflection and stabbing movement of this defense is a simulation of you diving into a pool, using your arms in a "V" motion, piercing through the water while maintaining a straightness to your legs. Your fingers should be together, touching at the fingertips to create an inverted "V" Make sure that your palms do not touch together. Drop one arm down into a straight punch position and align your deflect and redirect hand by leaning your body forward and dropping your chin into your shoulder.

This forward lean has two purposes. First, it will defeat the attack and second it will serve to protect your head. In essence, you are diving into your attacker using the left arm and leg to close up the distance, while counterstriking and deflecting the attack with the other.

Another way to look at this is to stand in a neutral position and punch your arm straight out to meet an incoming (imaginary) attack. To get your arm properly aligned, you should have a slight curve to the hand to intercept the attack. Keep your fingers tight together and your thumb tucked into the hand – if you allow the thumb to stick out, you run the risk of breaking it. When you time it right, this stabbing and deflecting defense will serve to redirect the weapon harmlessly over the top of your head, with a glance off your back.

You must time the defense and the counter punch together Step forward with your left leg, closing up the distance and make sure that you are leading with your hands. Redirect using one hand and counterpunch with the other hand.

As you move towards your attacker, take your deflecting and stabbing arm over the top of the weapon, without breaking your contact with his or her arm, and secure the weapon arm. Continue the counterattack using a foreleg kick or knee strikes to the groin- this will depend on the distance between you and your attacker.

The most popular way of removing an impact weapon is to use a 180-degree step, starting from your right foot, to rip the weapon out of his or her hands, without breaking eye contact.

When you are comfortable with this defense movement, try adding in a simultaneous punch with the other arm, punching both of your arms out together. Keep your palm down or at least parallel to the ground, and target the throat, jaw or nose.

Now, let's assume that your assailant is coming at you with a chair or a stool, with the intent of using it in an overhead swing attack. Close up the distance between you, aligning your stabbing and deflecting hand with a forward body lean. Make sure your chin is tucked into your shoulder. Explode towards your assailant with the opposite leg. Your hand should be slightly bent and this should land just above the hand holding the weapon. The attack will go over your head harmlessly and, at the same time, you should step forward with the rear leg. Make sure that your deflecting hand maintains contact with your attacker's arms, allowing the attack to go along your arm, harmlessly again, over your shoulder.

Turn the deflecting palm in and wrap it around the attacker's arm, using this to get control of the weapon. At the same time, counterattack with over the top elbow strikes or strong punches, combined with a few knee strikes.

If you cannot capture both of your attacker's arms, your goal should be to control the far side arm by gripping it in an overhand grp. If you have successfully gotten control of the weapon, use it as your own weapon, following the Krav Maga principle of using weapons of opportunity.

If both of you have lost control of the weapon, kick it away. This does not necessarily violate the principle of controlling the weapon at all time because, by kicking the weapon away, you are controlling it by the only means that you have at your disposal. If another attacker were then to pick that chair up, with the intent of using it against you, there is a control technique in Krav Maga that puts the original assailant directly in the line of fire. Worst case, you will have to defend yourself against another attack.

Next, we are going to look at defending against an attacker who is trying to stab you straight on.

This type of defense lets you deflect a stab, be it left or right handed, starting from a left or right stance, while at the same time stepping off the attack line, trapping your attackers arm and delivering counterpunches to the throat, nose or chin of the attacker. The same defense can be used against an eye gouge, straight punch or a front choke, one or two handed.

Standing in a regular left stance, your left arm leads the charge while you step to the side. Your arm should be bent at an angle of around 70 degrees in order to deflect the straight stab at the same time as sidestepping left. The parry movement with your left hand shouldn't be any more than four to six inches because this is what is responsible for leading the defense movement. The deflection is not meant to be a swipe at the attacker's arm in an uncontrolled movement – this is one of the most common mistakes made at the beginning of training. Your defense arm should make full use of the entire forearm, from your little finger to your elbow, to deflect the change of height in the stab. The movement will also rotate your wrist out so that your thumb turns away from you – do keep all your fingers pointing up and your thumb tucked in. This movement will help to redirect the stab. Make sure that contact with the attacker's weapon arm is maintained; even if you are unable to secure that arm, you can at least pin it to his or her body and continue with your counterattacks.

Do keep it in mind that your attacker may lunge, which will bring you into his or her dead side, closing up the distance while you step off the line. Once you have made the parry, maintaining that contact with the arm, which your attacker is most likely going to retract, you can hook the attackers arm by cupping your hand and wrapping your thumb around his or her forearm to control it; pin it against his or her torso, at the same time delivering counterpunches to his or her jaw or throat.

Note that, one again your assailant may lunge, bringing you into his or her dead side. However, regardless of what happens, do not break the contact with his or her arm and do not stop making your counterpunches. So long as you stay inside the arc of the attack, you will be safe.

While you are pushing your counterattack, you can use your right arm to control and secure the weapon arm, using a fishhook to the eye, a neck crank or another combative to take the attacker down.

If you can get your attacker into a headlock, you can take dominant control of the situation. You must be able to control the weapon and get yourself onto your attackers' dead side. Once you are there, reach round his or her head to make his chin and head secure against your body, while simultaneously using a 180 degree sidestep to take the attacker down. All the while, you must maintain control of the weapon.

Your goal is to avoid being stabbed while getting onto his or her dead side, simultaneously counterattacking. Include a powerful takedown, stomping the head and taking the weapon from his or her hand or you can turn the assailant over and restrain him while removing the weapon.

To take the weapon, put your right hand on the top of his or her right hand, knuckle to knuckle, and punch his or her wrist towards their body using the palm of your hand. Use your hips and your upper body together. To boost the power, let go of your grip to bend your arm slightly to deliver a palm heel strike to the wrist. You can also use an elbow strike to the wrist but do be careful that you do not get injured with the weapon. As you break the posture of the wrist, dig into his or her palm with your fingers, wrapping around the grip of the weapon, using your fingers to take the weapon.

Top 10 Krav Maga Moves

These 10 moves are good ways to defend against any kind of attack. The art of Krav Maga places emphasis on defense and attack as a continuous movement, in order to neutralize the attacker.

Kick to the Front

The aim of Krav Maga is to end an attack very quickly. Deliver a kick out to the front with your leg to provide more power, aiming for the abdomen, groin, head, knee or neck. Follow this up with strike from your elbow or a powerful punch to the rear of your attacker's neck.

Strike to the Eyes

This is a move that will temporarily blind your attacker. It is a useful move for women to use who are confronted by a strong attacker. Use your thumbs or your fingers to dig into the sockets of the eyes

Defending against a Person who Grabs the Buttocks

This is another good move, especially for women who are victims of harassment. If an assailant attacks from the rear, carry out a backward kick and aim for the groin or the knee. You could also use a backward strike with your elbow, and follow up with any Krav Maga movement, including a volley of hard punches or a front kick.

Side Kick While Stepping

This is one of the best moves to allow you to close the space between you rapidly and strike an attacker beside you. If your attacker is on the right, cross one leg over the other, move your weight to the other leg and twist your hips, kicking out with your heel. Aim for the shin, abdomen, knee and thigh.

One-Hit Punch

The main point to the art of Krav Maga is to block while simultaneously attacking an assailant. A one-hit punch, sometimes called a "Sucker Punch". Sucker punches are straight punches. If you need to deflect one, use the outside block and follow it with a knee or a hard punch to the kidneys.

Elbow Strike to the Rear

This is a great move for a rear attack. Make sure that your arms are parallel with the ground ensuring they are raised just above the level of your shoulders. Twist your hips as you strike your attacker using your knee.

Striking Upwards with the Elbow

This is an offensive move that is designed to deliver damage to the throat or shin of your attacker. Once you have gotten into a fighting stance, bend from the knees a little and deliver a strike upwards using your elbow.

Punching Upwards

Your fist is one of the deadliest weapons that you have and using it for an upward sharp punch can leave your attacker somewhat shaken, sufficient for you to be able to carry out another move very quickly. Aim for the chin and generate the power by bending your knee and twisting the hips as your fists land on the target.

Defending Against a Head Butt Attack

This s a very effective defensive move that is highly effective against a head butt. Bring your elbow up, keeping it in line with the ground and block off the face of your attacker while delivering a punch to the head using your opposite hand.

Defense Against a Choke from the Rear

While chokes are designed to render you unconscious, they take some time to be truly effective. Krav Maga teaches you to how to stay calm, to use your arms to get yourself free by grabbing pulling at your attacker's elbow. This is followed by sweeping up backwards and hooking his or her leg.

Chapter 7

Angry Training

Angry training is not training when you are angry about something; it is about teaching you how to deal with an attack from a person or persons who are clearly not going to be gentle about what they are doing. It is about teaching you how to deal with an angry person. The following guidelines are to be learned and practiced if you are to successfully fend off an attack.

- Before you do battle with an opponent, exhaust all other options first. Doing battle should be the absolute last course of action – don't get draw in to a physical fight if there is no need
- If your opponent shows no signs of stopping, get yourself into the correct battle stance. Turn your body sideways so that your dominant shoulder is facing your opponent. Raise your fists up to

guard your body and your head but not so that your vision is obstructed.

- Learn how to obstruct an attack. To stop a punch from making contact with you, open your hand and push the approaching fist away. You will most likely still get struck but you can deflect the punch away from an area that could cause you significant damage, such as your head, groin belly or kidneys

- Learn how to counterattack. Don't go for the "wild hook" type of punch, you know the one, where you throw your arm out in a big "C" shape. From your battle position, your punch has to come from the center of the body. It is natural to expect the punch to come in quick and for you to strike back quick so do not leave your arm out in the middle of nowhere, making it an easy target. You can kick out to avert an attack or do your own damage but remember that your kick has to come from the foot in the battle position. Raise your leg up and snap it out, bringing it back quickly, out of harm's way.

- You must learn the correct way to make a fist. This might seem like a stupid thing to have to learn; after all, we all know how to make a fist, don't we. However, what you have to understand is the right way to punch out with the fit in the right position to stop you from hurting yourself. Make a fit now; I will pretty much guarantee that your fingers are curled in and your thumb is either wrapped around the top of your index finger or tucked underneath your fingers. Both are incorrect positions and both can lead to a broken thumb. You must position your thumb around your fingers, and rest it on or below the middle and index fingers. Also remember to keep your wrist straight when you toss a punch out as this can also stop you from hurting yourself

- Give the appearance of being strong. Your posture is vital here; you must keep your back straight and keep a reasonable rate of strolling. If you appear to be hurrying or darting about, you will look suspicious and you will look scared. Confidence is everything. Hold your head up high and, if you are walking through an area that is potentially dangerous, don't avert your eyes from anyone around you. Look them straight in the eye but remain fully concentrated on where you are. This achieves three things – first, it tells people that you are aware of what is around you and on the lookout for danger.

Second, it allows you to speak to people if you need or want to, without sounding or looking scared, and third, it allows you to acknowledge and recognize certain individuals in the vicinity. All of this leads to a more confident outlook and you are less likely to be attacked by just anyone.

- Always be aware of where you are. Attackers often approach victims in quiet location and at night when there are less people about. Always be aware of what is going on around you and keep an eye out for anyone who may look to be approaching you
- Always be on the defensive. If you spot someone who is making a clear path towards you with the obvious intention of attacking, stand with your feet firm and slightly apart, and your back and head held firm and straight. Command them to stop in a loud voice. This will make you look strong, confident and sure of what you are doing and, in many cases, this is enough to avert a potential attack. If the person approaching stops but doesn't make any move to leave, then speak to them confidently, asking them if they are following you, why they are following you, what is it they want. Try to ascertain what their objectives are and what their intent is but do

maintain your confident stance. If you get a response, try to encourage them to leave you alone or come to some kind of compromise. If necessary, if they want money, you may have to give it to them to leave you alone. It is far better to lose your money than it is to put your life at risk.

- If the individual will not back down and will not leave you alone, instantly go into a combat position. If you are a right handed person, step your right foot behind you, left foot if you are left handed. Do not step too far back as tis will severely limit your range of movement and can easily put you off balance. The best position is to place your foot a shoulder width behind. This is your pillar from which to attack should your aggressor push against you – it will most certainly prevent you from falling backwards. That is the last thing you want – as soon as you hit the floor, on your back, it will all be over. This is a kind of boxing position, with your foot behind you just a little bit more. This rear foot an also be used as a way of attacking with a kick as well. With your dominant foot in the rear position, hold out your non-dominant arm in front of your face with your fists clenched in the right way. This is the arm that will work to protect you and help to deflect off an attack. Your dominant arm should be positioned a bit lower, ready for attack, meaning that any fit aiming for your face can almost certainly be deflected, allowing you the space to kick out.

- Grab for your attacker's hair or head with your dominant attacking hand and then bring your safeguard foot up, lowering your attackers head and hitting it against your bent knee. This should all be one smooth fluid movement. If you can do this properly, you will almost certainly surprise or stop them for enough time to make your escape.

- Throw a well-aimed punch at your attacker's nose. This will serve to confuse them, may break their nose and will give you enough time to escape. When you do punch out, shout out loudly as this reinforce the attack and it will surprise your attacker. It will also grab his attention. If you do need to do this, throw all your force behind it, enough to make a difference. A weak punch will do nothing for you and it may make your attacker even more angry. You must punch as though your life depended on it, which, at this stage, it may well do.

- If you are attacked from behind, a very likely scenario, and the attacker grabs you and wraps their arms around your chest and waist, tug hard to free your arms completely. When your attacker grabs you like this their head will be close to one shoulder so, using the arm that is on the same side as their head, strike your elbow back hard into their face. As they go backwards, grab hold of their arm and free yourself sufficiently to step forwards, allowing you an escape route.
- After you step forwards, step back again quickly and then side to side. In effect you are literally shaking off your attacker and knocking him or her off balance, to the extent that you can perform a move that throws them over your shoulder. This will work better if they are taller than you. Practice this one in safety before you attempt it for real.
- If your attacker grabs your arm with their hand, flatten your fingers out a much as you and pull against where their fingers are. By making your and flat you are stiffening up the bones in your arm, which makes it easier to get out of their grasp, even if they are stronger and more powerful than you are.

The final thing to remember is, if someone jumps you, try not to get thrown to the ground as you will not be able to defend yourself very well and will find yourself at the mercy of your attacker.

Chapter 8

Defending Yourself with These Three Moves

Self-defense is an important skill to learn and the three moves I am going to tell you about are key. However, you should only every apply these when you are in a real situation of duress. Remember that when you are in a position of danger and you have to fight back with force, always aim for a soft target – your attacker's nose, eyes, jaw ears, groin, throat, pubic bone, knees and Achilles tendon. Striking at these areas can inflict some serious damage on your attacker and must only be used when the situation absolutely calls for it and there is no other way.

Familiarize yourself with these moves; not only can they perhaps save your life one day, they can also help to strengthen your body and your mind.

Defending Yourself Against a One-Handed Choke Up Against a Wall

The attacker will use one hand to grab you by the throat, holding on and pushing you against a wall

Note - This attack is designed to ensure that you comply with what the attacker wants. One thing that could give you the advantage is to act as if you are compliant and are not resisting; this will give you a chance to break free of the hold quickly so that your attacker hasn't got enough time to make use of the other hand, either to choke you or to grab a weapon. This is your chance to get a strike in.

- Tuck in your chin, down towards your chest. This will pressure on your opponent's thumb and will weaken his or her hold.
- Raise up your hands, open your palms close to his or her wrist. Use your non-dominant hand to grab hold of their wrist, near to the thumb and remove it from your throat in a plucking option, i.e., drive it downwards, towards the ground. At

the same time, raise your dominant hand and strike out at his or her nose, throat or jaw.

- As you strike, pivot your hips into the move to add more force and momentum, making your punch more powerful
- Continue with your knee into his or her groin area and continue striking out at the recommended soft spots

Defending Yourself Against a Knife to the Throat Attack from the Rear

The attacker will approach you from behind, placing a knife to your throat while using the other hand to hold your arm and control your movement, limiting you.

Note – This kind of attack is deemed to be the ultimate in convincing you to comply with them. There is a very real danger of death here and most people will do pretty much anything to avoid it. This is why this kind of attack is used so much.

- Give the impression that you are not resisting and are complying fully with your opponent's demands. Do not make any movement initially because it could result in the knife cutting your throat, accidentally or otherwise

- In one swift move, place your hands on to your attacker's wrist, the one holding the knife, and pull down their arm, keeping it in close to your chest. Drop your whole weight down, tuck in your chin and look at the blade, or toward it. This takes the threat away from your throat and to your face, which, although bad enough, is nowhere near as deadly.
- Strike at your attackers going using your nearest hand and then quickly take your hand back to restrain their wrist
- Your opponent should still have his or her arm wrapped round your throat and you should be a little off to their right side Tuck in your head underneath their armpit, making sure your chin stays down and you still have their knife hand secured. Turn your body and feet so that you are to the side of your attacker instead of your bac to his front.
- Step on his foot hard and shove him or her to the ground.

Defending Yourself Against a Stomp Kick to the Groin

The attacker will kick you or knee you in the groin or midsection, which may lead to very serious damage, very agonizing pain and leave you open to more attacks.

Note - If your opponent kicks out using his or her right leg, defend using your left hand and vice versa. This will also work for many other defensive moves. This will mean that your arm can be kept as straight as possible so that your forearm, swiping cross your body, will give you maximum coverage and provide protection.

- When your attacker starts to raise his or her leg to bring their knee up, use your opposite or mirror hand to divert it by swiping your arm across your body as mentioned above. Use your entire arm length to do this, don't just grab out at their leg
- Step sideways, moving away from the direction his or her leg is moving in. This will put you either at their back or side
- Strike out at their face with a closed fist as soon as you have blocked their move.

Chapter 9

5 Krav Maga Moves To Devastate and Dominate

These 5 Krav Maga moves are powerful enough to give you the edge over your opponent. Learn them and you can be calm and confident in the face of adversity.

Krav Maga is full of effective fighting move but there are only a small number that are worth spending any real time learning. These are 5 of the very best moves that will help you to defend yourself when you are caught, unawares and alone, on a dark street at night.

The Knee Strike

This is a great move to practice with a partner who is holding a training pad against their lower chest. Done right, you can produce an awful lot of power. Grab hold of your attacker's head on both sides and pull him down firmly. At the same time, strike your knee up and into his stomach or solar plexus. If you can bring him down low enough with your hand, you can also aim for the ribs. Knee repeatedly until your attacker is on the floor or can do you no further harm.

Elbow Strike

Like many other marital arts, Krav Maga teaches you how to use the hard parts of your body against the soft parts of your attacker. This is the best way for you to hurt your attacker and avoid being hurt yourself. You can use your elbow in a number of ways:

- **Vertically** – Using a sweeping motion, move your bent arm rapidly from your side to up by your head. When you practice, you should find that your wrist is beside your ear on the same side as the arm you are going to use for striking, just like you were answering the phone. This strike will come up underneath the chin of your attacker and knock him or her out.
- **Horizontally** – Sweep your arm from right to left or left to right, moving your arm across your body at the same height all the way. You will use your upper back or chest muscle to add more power to the strike. This attack normally targets

the head of the attacker, hitting the temple or jaw area
- **Diagonally** – You use this one in a slashing or chopping movement, from right up to right down, down low to up, left to right and right to left. This strike is a sharp glancing one that aim for the head of your attacker and can result in a broken jaw or a knockout

Always follow up a strike with other moves. Feel free to repeat the technique over and over if it works, if it can knock your opponent to the ground or, if needs be, switch to another technique altogether. Keep in mind that it is sometime more effective to repeat a technique over and over if it is working, rather than hanging to see if something else might be more effective.

Palm Strike

This is a very easy Krav Maga more to learn and is also one of the most powerful. It is a common move across many different fighting systems and there is a good reason for that – it works. You can use the palm strike like a boxing punch but, instead of using a fist, you open up your hand and strike with the bottom portion of your hand, the thickest part near to the wrist.

This is a pretty strong area that won't hurt too much if you hit hard or bony parts of your opponent, like their skull or chin. You should aim this up under the chin and follow it through by pretending that you are attempting to send his head up through a roof – this will probably result in you knocking him or her out. This is an extremely powerful move and a very effective one. You don't actually need vast amounts of strength to knock a person out as all you are doing is knocking their chin straight up, which effectively and suddenly kinks the back of their neck.

The head is the absolute best target for this, just like it is for many Krav Maga moves. You can use a palm strike against the body but the shape of an open hand is not really conducive to a body strike. However, the palm strike can help to protect your knuckles from being broken or damaged when you strike the head of your opponent.

Knife Hand Strike

This is another Krav Maga move that is used in many other martial arts for the exact same reason as the palm strike – because it is so effective. The easiest and best way to form a knife strike hand is something you have probably seen many times in the movies. Simply extend your fingers out as if you are about to shake the hand of your opponent, but keep your thumb tucked against your index finger instead of extending it upright. When you strike, tighten up your wrist and fingers and make sure that you use the meaty part of your palm at the base of your little finger.

This is the second hardest and toughest part of your hand, second only to the base of the palm. Do make sure that you don't strike your attacker with your little finger or you run the risk of breaking it. Also, you can't it with any real force with your little finger at the point of impact; all it will do is give way.

You can direct this move against any part of the attacker's body but the bet spots to aim for are the sides of the head and the throat or anywhere on the front of the neck. If you are behind your attacker or he is bent over, go for the back of the neck, near the base of his or her skull.

You can also use the knife hand strike to chop at your attacker's forearms if he or she attempts to grab you or has already grabbed you. If your other arm is being held, you could use the move to chop at their forearm to make them you go.

Follow this straightaway with a sweeping knife and strike to the side of the head or neck and remember to keep on hitting until your attacker is down or is no longer attempting to hurt you. Don't hit once and then stand at look at him or her – they will most likely come straight back at you and attack harder. Relentless and tough, that is the key with this, the only way to break your attacker and stop them from coming for you again.

Break Falls

The final move is to learn how to fall safely, i.e. in a way that doesn't break any of your bones. You might find it odd to fall on purpose but this is one of the first things that any martial art will teach you. Practice on soft mats or grass first, so you can get the hang of it.

There are a number of different types of break fall:

- Forward roll
- Backward roll
- Back break fall
- Side break fall

The one thing that they all have in common with each other is that they all teach you how to fall in a controlled manner so that you don't run any risk of being hurt.

When you practice them enough your body will automaticity go straight into one of them, the right one for the situation and you won't even think about doing it. All of these moves ae highly effective at helping to protect you when you all over, be it accidentally or because someone has taken you down.

Chapter 10

Krav Maga Belts

There is no doubt that the Israeli form of self-defense, Krav Maga, is quite possibly the deadliest martial art in use today. It does se concepts from other martial arts, like Aikido, Jujitsu, Judo, Boxing, Muay Thai, Wing Chun and many others. The bet system for Krav Maga is also based on that of the Judo belt system.

If you are planning to get to grips with Krav Maga, then you have to learn the belt and grading system. This is the structure you will need to follow as you improve and advance. A Krav Maga student will always be striving to get the next bet, the next level up from the one they are currently on, always keeping a firm eye on their goals.

This kind of system has always served Judo and Karate very well and it also works for Krav Maga. The ranking system ensures that students work as hard as they possibly can to master the true art of Krav Maga and work their way up through the ranks.

Krav Maga Belts and Ranking System

RANK LEVEL	BELT COLOR
Beginner	White
Level 1	Yellow
Level 2	Orange
Level 3	Green
Level 4	Blue
Level 5	Brown
Level 5	Black

The Basics of the Krav Maga Belt Structure

As I said earlier, the belt system is based on the Judo system, Judo being the very first of the martial arts to make use of a belt system to rank students from beginner right up to expert level. However, traditionally, Judo only used the belt colors of black and white.

It wasn't until it entered Europe that things changed and western schools added in more colors to the belt and grading system. With the addition of the different colors, students were now certain of their stance in terms of skill and experience and they now had a visible goal to reach for.

Krav Maga took on the Western Judo style of grading and now uses seven colors of belt and three categories which are identified by way of a patch on the Krav Maga uniform:

- Practitioner Level 1 - White Belt
- Practitioner Level 2 and Level 3 - Yellow Belt
- Practitioner Level 4 and Level 5 - Orange Belt
- Practitioner Level 6 and Graduate Level 1 - Green Belt
- Graduate Level 2 and Level 3 - Blue Belt
- Graduate Level 4 and Level 5 - Brown Belt
- Expert Level 1 to Level 5 - Black Belt

There is also one more category beyond expert, known as Master Level. Very few people have ever attained Master Level and those that have are generally those who have spent their entire lives contributing to and furthering the future of Krav Maga

Moving to the Next Belt

Moving to the next belt require 3 main things from a student:

- Time

- The mastery of a number of specific techniques

- The completion of a set syllabus

The time it will take to move up from one belt to the next differs from school to school. Normally, you should expect it to take between 12 and 24 months to advance in Practitioner category and at least 24 months to advance through graduate category.

To qualify for the green and the blue belt, and to officially enter the Graduate category, the Practitioner has to pass a test that shows they have completely mastered all of the skills in the Practitioner levels, as well as the techniques. They must also work through a syllabus that proves they have learned all that comes within the Practitioner level as well. The test may be a written one or it may be a verbal test before a panel of Expert Krav Maga instructors.

Graduates and Instructors

Civilian Krav Maga instructors are usually Graduates who have attained Brown belt level. They have passed their instructor exams and this mean that all Krav Maga instructors are Graduates but, conversely, not all Graduates are instructors.

Those who advance to Expert and wear the Black belt are so far advanced that they generally teach the skills to the military and at police academies. These are the people who teach Israeli soldiers to use advanced war combat skills instead of the techniques that are used for the competitive sport.

Krav Maga Master also wear the black belt but of a different design. They do not teach as much but run schools instead. There are very few people who have attained this level.

Getting to the Black Belt

There is one more thing you need to know about obtaining a black belt and advancing to Expert level – you must be invited. The other belts just require the student to be at a specific belt for a certain time and then pass a test in skills in order to move up; the black belt is purely invitation only.

What this means is that only those who have advanced beyond brown belt levels are considered to be experts by the martial arts society. Those students are extended an invitation to hold the black belt because they have shown true dedication, time, real loyalty and real skill in the art of Krav Maga.

In most Krav Maga schools, the level of the black belts is split into 9 degrees or dans. These 9 are then further divided into 5 levels and moving up through the levels also requires an invitation to be extended.

Krav Maga gradings are not totally necessary but they are a great way for you to set your goals and a real way of measuring how well you are improving. They are a way of helping you to grow your levels of knowledge, of testing out how you apply the principles of Krav Maga, the strategies.

During a grading you may find yourself running a whole range of emotions, from a little discomfort, through joy and total fear, to euphoria, anxiety and even down to struggling for breath through panic. In a nutshell you are likely to have a mix of both negative and positive feelings.

This is totally natural as it is our own bodies helping us to cope with the experience we are going through. You must acknowledge any of the emotions for what they truly are – a chemical reaction inside your body, and accept that it is a natural thing. However, if you do go for grading and you do find yourself acting very differently to the way you would normally, it is important to remember not to panic, especially if you feel very uncomfortable and start to make mistakes where you wouldn't normally. Part of the test is learning to be uncomfortable with being uncomfortable, if that makes sense, and you will grow to be a much stronger person as a result of it.

Keeping that in mind, the following tips will help you with your grading:

Pre Grading:

- Do not limit your own belief. If you believe that you are going to pass or you believe that you are going to fail, it's almost certain that you will. Some people see the examiners as the enemy and believe that they are going to be failed no matter what they do. You must stop believing like this – if you have been training properly and regularly, your grading should be nothing different to another training day.
- Practice hard and practice as much as you can. Always go to the grading practice sessions and have a good look through the curriculum – make sure you understand everything that is expected

of you. Take notes on the techniques and brush up on those that you are unsure of. If you need help with a certain part before the grading, ask for it, don't try to struggle on alone.

During Grading:

- Make sure that your kicks and punches are fast and make extra sure that you bring them back even quicker

- Move away from the line. When you have done a technique, move away from the line and start passive scanning. As soon as you have moved, stay away from the spot that you began from and pick the best way to either advance or to retreat.

- Active scanning. As soon as you have completed a technique, carry out a 360-degree scan of the room. This is different from passive scanning, where just a quick glance is needed.

- Be choosy but be specific about where you strike when you are countering an attack. Keep in mind that most people are going to expect you to strike at their face so go for the groin as well, using a proper Krav Maga method for the distance involved. Don't be patting anyone on the back after you have done this, save it for after the grading

- Keep on going. Do not under any circumstances, give up. I know it is easy for a viewer to say this but you must carry on or you will fail. Teach yourself a mantra to chant in your mind, to get you through timed drills especially if your energy and mental reserves are fast emptying out

- Scan all the time. You must always be aware of what I going on about you while remaining focused on your goals. You never know when an attack may come from where you least expect.

Post Grading:

- Eat. Have something nice but nutritious with you to munch on after your grading – you'll need it.

- Thank your examiner and any representative of the MG that may be present. Thank them for taking the time to put you through all the mad stuff you just did and for taking the time to test your skills. No matter whether you pass or whether you fail, the examiner does not have anything personal against you. Take their feedback and learn from it.

Chapter 11

The Language of Krav Maga

As you advance through Krav Maga, you will come across these common terms; in fact, you will have seen some of them in this book. As soon as you learn and understand the language of Krav Maga, you will have a better understanding of the method and the techniques -

Combative - Any type of strike, throw, takedown, choke, joint lock, or any other type of offensive fight move

Retzev - This is a Hebrew word that refers to "continuous motion in combat". It is the true backbone of the modern Israeli fighting technique and it teaches you how to move on instinct when you are caught up in combat motion, without having to consciously think of your next move. When you find yourself in a dangerous situation, you will automatically fall back on your physical and mental training to launch a counterattack, a seamless and overwhelming attack that makes use of all sorts of offensive or combative actions combined with taking evasive action. Retzev is a decisive movement, a quick one that merge every aspect of your training. Defense transitions to offence in a bid to neutralize the attack on you, giving your attacker very little time to react or respond.

Left outlet stance - Turning your feet by approximately 30 degrees to the right blades your body, with your left leg and left arm forward Doing the opposite, i.e. turning your feet right puts you on the right outlet stance. you should be resting on the ball of the rear foot and you should be in a balanced comfortable position. Your feet must be parallel and around 55% of your body weight should be distributed over the front leg. The arms are in front of your face, bent with a 60 degree angle in between the upper and forearms. From this stance, you can move forwards, backwards and sideways and move your feet in concert with one another.

Live side - When you face your opponent front on, he or she can see you and can use both legs and arms against you. This is the live side.

Dead side – The opposite of the live side, this when you are behind your attacker's near shoulder or are facing his or her back. You are in the most advantageous of positions and can easily counterattack and take control of your attacker. He or she cannot use their arms or legs very easily to attack. Always move to the dead side whenever you can; this also serves to put your attacker in between you and any other attackers that may be coming.

Same side - This is where same-side arm and leg face your opponent. For example, if you face your attacker with your left side opposite his or her right side, your same side is your left arm, opposite his or her right.

Near side - The limb on your attacker that is closest to your torso

Outside defense - outside defense is used to counter outside attack, i.e. an attack directed at you from the outside to the inside of your body. Two examples of outside attacks are a hook punch and a slap on the face.

Inside defense - Inside defense defends against the straight or inside attack. These attacks include punching a person in the face or poking a finger into their eye, or any other thrusting motion.

Gunt - This is the absorption or deflection of a strike done by bending your elbow so that your bicep touches the forearm. The angle of the deflection will depend entirely on the type and angle of the strike. For example, if a hook punch is thrown at you or a roundhouse kick aimed at the head, you would bend your elbow and position it to protect your head, keeping the back of your arm parallel with the ground and the tip of your elbow pointing outward a little.

You can also use the gunt as a defense against a knee attack, by jamming the tip of your elbow into your attacker's knee.

Glicha - This is a sliding movement, done on the balls of the feet and carrying your whole body weight forward and through a strike as a way of giving the maximum impact

Secoul - A larger version of the Glicha, moving over a larger distance and carrying your body through a strike with the maximum amount of impact.

Off angle - An angle of attack that is no directly face to face

Stepping off the line - using a combination of body and footwork to take evasive action when faced with a linear attack, like a kick or a straight punch. This may also be termed ass "breaking the angle of an attack".

Tsai - bake - a semi-circle step, usually 180 degrees, done by rotating a leg back, creating a certain amount of torque on the joint to finish off a control hold or a complete takedown

Cavalier - Otherwise known as a "wrist takedown" where you force your attackers wrest to move outside of its natural motion range. You would normally combine this with tsai-bake to provide more power

Trapping - This happens when you grab your attacker's arms or pin them using one arm, leaving you with one arm free to continue striking

Figure four - This is a control hold that secures your attackers arm, or torso in order to exert pressure. The hold is enabled by using both arms on the joint of the tendon, shoulder or wrist of your attacker.

Mount - The mount is a formidable control and fight position where you straddle your attacker so his or her back is to the ground and your heels hooked in under their rib cage

Rear mount - The best control position when fighting on the ground. You are behind your attacker and straddling him or her with your legs around their midsection, wrapped not crossed.

Side mount - This is a position of strong control where you have your right knee pressed into your attacker's hip and left knee in complete line with his or her head. The elbow that is closest to your attacker's head should be on his or her ear.

Knee on stomach - This is another very strong position of control where you place your entire weight on your attacker's midsection, and hook your foot into his or her hip, while remaining on the ball of your foot, creating a stable platform for striking from and wearing down your attacker's body.

Side control - Your attacker is on his or her back and you are seated, legs splayed, and controlling his or her head and the arm loses to you with your arm

High closed guard - You have your back to the round and your attacked is trapped between your legs, and your ankles are hooked together.

Kicking pad - This is a large shield, made of foam, that is deigned to be used for training purposes, held

104

by a partner while you practice your knee strikes and kicks

Hand pad or muy Thai pad - a foam pad that is maneuverable and designed to be held by a partner while you train and practice your punches, elbow strikes and other upper body strikes.

Krav Maga

Chapter 12

Krav Maga FAQ

Finally, I want to go over some of the more frequently asked questions about Krav Maga training.

Where Can I learn Krav Maga?

Krav Maga is taught at professional classes all over the world and there are more and more centers opening every day. Simply check your local directory or the internet for the nearest classes to you.

What Do I Wear to a Class?

The most important thing is that you are comfortable so wear a t-shirt, tracksuit trousers and training shoes. Your instructors and regular students will wear an official KMG uniform, which consists of a black t-shirt that has a white logo on it (red for instructors) and black trousers that are similar to those worn in kickboxing, again with a logo.

Do I Need to Take Anything Else to Class with Me?

Yes, you must have some form of groin protection. Safety is always the first priority of any Krav Maga class and accidents very rarely happen. However, being punched or kicked in the groin is not nice, whether it was an accident or intentional. You can get a sports groin guard from any sports supply shop but you should go for the martial art type if you can.

Also bring a towel and plenty of fresh water.

What Can I Expect from a Typical Krav Maga Class?

Class opening.

The instructor will ask all students to form a line and he will welcome you all to the training. You will be asked to bow in Hebrew (the word is "kida"). This is the only formal type of etiquette in the martial art.

Warm up. This is about 15 to 25 minutes of light cardiovascular work, stretching, joint oiling, power exercises and, in some classes, a game. Even in this part, you will be learning some Krav Maga.

Introduction to individual or a group of techniques. Your instructor will talk about the theme of the specific class and will then introduce the technique for the lesson. Every technique will be demonstrated a number of times at full speed, a number of times in slow motion and then again with detailed explanations of how to do it.

You are the given a chance to "dry drill" each technique, working on body ad motor skills. Following this is a "body drill". With a partner, you will slowly practice the moves, building up speed at your own pace. Last is the "summary drill", which is where you get the opportunity to practice each technique in a way that is as real as possible without any danger.

Final exercise. This is normally some kind of game or exercise that covers the new skills you have learned. It will be safe but it will also be challenging at the same time. It lets you find any areas where you might need more practice.

Stretching. Depending on what you cover in the class, there may be a little stretching at the end, just so you don't feel stiff or sore the next day.

Closing. This is the same as the start; all students line up, bow (kida) and give a round of applause.

Do I Have to be Really Fit to do Krav Maga?

No, absolutely not. Krav Maga is all about self-defense, realistic defense that is aimed at anyone and everyone. One of the bones to Krav Maga training is that your fitness levels will improve. However, this is not the goal for the class and you will be encouraged to progress at your own level.

I Don't Do Martial Arts and Never Have. Can I Still do Krav Maga?

Yes. In most cases it is actually an advantage not to have any martial arts background because you won't be tempted to fall into old ways or have to unlearn what you learnt already.

Will it Hurt?

We hope not. Safety is the number one priority in any class and, although there's always a risk, provided you listen to your instructor and follow instructions properly, those risks are negligible. You will also find that your instructor will be a fully qualified first aider.

You will need to get insurance before you start – this is mandatory and covers you for Public Liability, Member to Member Liability and Personal Accident Liability. Your instructor can provide you with details.

What will I Learn at Krav Maga?

One of the most essential parts of Krav Maga is the methods, teaching process and the style of training. KM instructors undergo seriously intensive training and keep up to date. They are also experienced teachers in other forms of protection and self-defense. Some of the subjects you will learn are:

- Avoidance, prevention, evasion and escape
- Dealing with falls and throws, all angles and all directions
- Attacks and counterattacks. These are performed on all different targets, ranges, heights, distances and directions. They are also executed from all posture and positions and using all kind of common object for the purpose of defense.
- Defending unarmed attacks, including strikes, punches and kicks as well as releases from all types of holds and grabs
- Defense against armed attack, including knife and any sharp object, bars, sticks and any other form of blunt instruments, and firearms
- Defense in all different types of place, including open areas and closed areas, all ground types and in the water

- Dense in all postures and positions including, free or limited movement, standing, moving, sitting, lying or facing downwards.
- Mental physical control and disarm

Chapter 13

So You Want to Learn Krav Maga

Krav Maga is a simple martial art. The premise of Krav Maga is to do exactly what it takes to ensure your own personal safety, to be aggressive and to use your own instinct. Here are the four things you need to do as a beginner in Krav Maga:

Learn Everything about Krav Maga

Before you begin, you have to get your mind around the concept of Krav Maga. This is especially important if you are already trained in other martial arts, as you need to break your conceptions of what it is all about.

- Watch as many videos as you can

- Read as many books about Krav Maga as you can

- Research the internet

- Go and watch some training sessions

Set Your Goal for Training

You must have a goal otherwise you will be destined to fail or to become nothing more than a mediocre fighter. Why are you training in Krav Maga? Is it to feel safer? Do you want to train towards becoming a Krav Maga instructor? Is it just a hobby? Write down exactly what you want to achieve.

Find a Training Facility

The best way to train is to go to your nearest licensed Krav Maga facility. By getting your training in person, as opposed to watching DVD's, you will have the motivation to continue, an expert there to help correct any mistakes you make, friends to practice with and people to encourage you.

By all means, watch DVD's as well. These are helpful because you can at least slow them down and watch the moves being made in slow motion, enabling you to study them properly. Do look to see if you can go and watch a few training sessions or take up a free trial session at your nearest facility as well.

Practice Constantly and Punch Through Your Opponent

This is a very important point. If you are already trained in martial arts, like karate or judo, you have developed some bad habits that need to be broken. These bad habits will prove to be highly counterintuitive to your Krav Maga training. For example, if you are practicing one-step sparring, normal sparring, katas or kumite, you will more than likely throw out the techniques but stop before you actually make contact with your opponent. This is to show that you have control and can demonstrate the art of the specific technique.

In Krav Maga, flashy techniques are thrown out of the window, along with perfect flawless execution. In Krav Maga, it is more important that you are aggressive and have brash reactions to a situation. When you are practicing delivering punches to the face, make sure that you punch through the top of your opponent's shoulder, making your hand go past the required distance to the rear of their skull. Your forearm should rub past their shoulder. This lets you practice the full speed, the full extension of power without actually hurting your opponent.

Remember – in Krav Maga, you practice your moves in the way you would execute them in a real life situation. You are not training for show; you are training to save your life.

Conclusion

I would like to thank you for taking the time to download and read my book. I hope it has been of some help to you and has given you some insight into what Krav Maga is and how it can help you.

Like any form of defense, you do need to be physically fit and in top form for it to be effective. And like anything, you must practice and practice hard. I can only tell you so much in this book; to become a true master at the art of Krav Maga you should attend proper training classes and watch as many videos as you can. Training classes will teach you the true art of Krav Maga in safety and will teach you the proper stances to avoid injuring yourself.

Once again, thank you for downloading my book and may I wish you good luck in your journey to learning the perfect art of self-defense.

Made in the USA
San Bernardino, CA
10 May 2016